Humans and Animals

Senses

David and Penny Glover

Smart Apple Media

First published in 2004 by Franklin Watts
96 Leonard Street, London EC2A 4XD

Franklin Watts Australia
45-51 Huntley Street, Alexandria NSW 2015

Series editor: Sally Luck, Art director: Jonathan
Hair, Design: Matthew Lilly

All photographs taken by Ray Moller unless
otherwise credited.

Acknowledgements : R. Austing/FLPA: front cover r,
11c; G. J. Cambridge/NHPA: 21b; James Carmichael
Jr./NHPA: 9br; Phillip Colla/Ecoscene: 13l; Manfred
Danegger/NHPA: 7tr; Delpho/Still Pictures: 11b;
Reinhard Dirsheri/Ecoscene: 25t; Clive Druett/Ecoscene:
21t; Pierre Gleizes/Still Pictures: 19t; Roger de la
Harpe/Still Pictures: 9t; Martin Harvey/NHPA: 23b.
David Lucas (www.dclvisions.com): 18;
Brian Mitchell/Photofusion: 14t, 16;
B.Odeur/Still Pictures: 13r; Robert Pickett/Ecoscene: 7tl,
17t, 19b; F Ravendam/Minden/FLPA: 17b; Jeffrey
Rotman/Still Pictures: 23t; Roland Seitre/Still Pictures:
7b; Albert Visage/Still Pictures: 15b, 25b; Konrad
Wothe/Minden/FLPA: 15t.

Published in the United States by Smart Apple
Media
2140 Howard Drive West, North Mankato,
Minnesota 56003

Library of Congress Cataloging-in-Publication Data

Glover, David, 1953 Sept. 4-
The senses / by David and Penny Glover.
p. cm. – (Humans and animals)
Includes index.
ISBN 1-58340-692-1
1. Senses and sensation–Juvenile literature. I.
Glover, Penny. II. Title.

QP434.G56 2005
612.8–dc22   2004052520

9 8 7 6 5 4 3 2 1

Contents

What are the senses?

Our five senses are smelling, tasting, feeling, hearing, and seeing.

We use our senses to explore the world around us.

Open a cold soda pop.
Can you see it?
Hear it? Feel it?
Smell it? Taste it?

Like humans, other animals use their senses to explore. A hungry fox smells a rabbit, then sees it in the grass. The rabbit hears the fox and stamps a warning to other rabbits.

A kiwi has tiny eyes, so it cannot see very well. To find food, it pokes the ground with its long bill. Its bill helps it smell worms and feel them move.

How do we see?

We see with our eyes.

Humans have two eyes. They are on our face, so we can see in front of us and a little to the side. We have to turn our heads and bodies to see around us.

Like a human, a crocodile has two eyes, but they are on top of its head. The crocodile can see above the water as it swims toward its prey.

Hold up a finger and look at it. Shut one eye at a time. Does the finger move? Two eyes help us see where things are.

Some animals have more than two eyes. This spider has eight eyes. Two main eyes at the front look for food. The other eyes look around for danger—like a hungry lizard or bird!

9

Can we see in the dark?

No.
We need light to see.

At night, the sky grows dark. Outside, the moon and stars give us a little light, but we also use street lamps and flashlights to help us see. Inside, we turn on electric lights.

Look in the mirror.
Close your eyes.
Your pupils get bigger
in the dark. Now open your
eyes and watch them get small again!

An owl has powerful eyes. It hunts at night and can see small animals in the grass. If we had eyes like owls, they would be as big as tennis balls!

A mole has tiny eyes. Like humans, it cannot see in the dark. It finds its way underground by touch and smell.

How do we hear?

We hear with our ears.

Sounds are all around us. We have two ears to help us tell where sounds come from. Our ears help us dance along to music!

Close your eyes and listen. Hold up a finger each time you hear a different sound. Can you count 10 sounds?

The blue whale is the biggest animal in the world. It sings underwater to talk to other whales. Blue whales can hear each other singing hundreds of miles away!

Bats use their ears to hunt in the dark. They make clicking sounds that bounce back to them from other animals, like moths. When they hear these echoes, they can catch their prey.

Can we all hear the same sounds?

No. We do not all hear the same sounds.

Some people have good hearing, but others cannot hear well. They talk using their hands. This is called sign language.

We use sign language when we wave hello or good-bye. What other signs do you use? Can you learn some new ones?

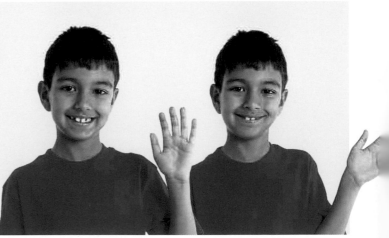

Snails do not have ears, so they cannot hear. They use their other senses to find food and stay safe.

An aardvark has very large ears. Its hearing is so good that it can hear ants walking underground. It listens carefully, then digs the ants out and eats them!

How do we feel?

We feel with our skin.

Our skin feels if something is hard or soft, rough or smooth, wet or dry. Fingertips are very sensitive. This girl is blind. She can read Braille. She feels the letters with her fingertips.

Some animals feel with special body parts. A cat has whiskers. Whiskers help it feel its way in the dark.

A sea anemone looks like a plant but it is an animal. It feels with its tentacles. When a small fish touches them, the sea anemone stings it, drags it to its mouth, and eats it.

17

Can we feel heat?

Yes. Our skin feels if something is hot or cold.

The water in a baby's bath must not be too hot or too cold. An adult tests the water first and puts the baby in when it feels just right.

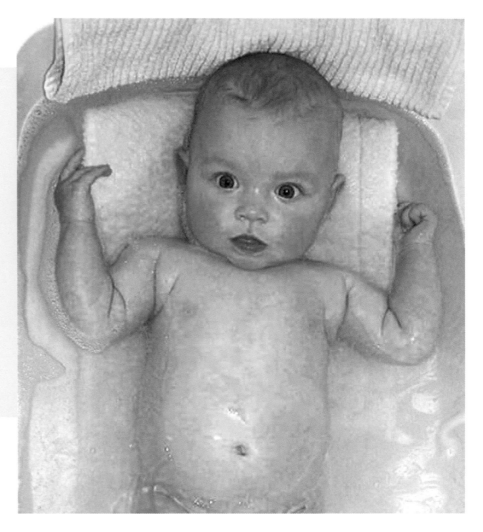

How long does it take you to get used to a cold swimming pool? Does it feel different when you get out, then get back in again?

Seals do not feel cold on icy land. Thick layers of fat and fur keep their bodies warm.

Some snakes have special pits in the skin under their eyes. The pits can sense the warmth of a nearby mouse. This helps the snakes hunt in the dark.

How do we smell?

We smell with our noses.

We breathe in through our nose to sniff smells. Smells can be good or bad. We enjoy good smells, but bad smells can warn us of danger.

What smells do you like? What smells don't you like? Ask your friends and make a "Top 10 Smells" list.

Bears have long noses. This means they can smell better than humans can. A bear can smell honey more than three miles (5 km) away!

Some animals smell with different body parts. A male moth smells with its feathery antennae. It can smell a female moth more than a mile (1.6 km) away.

Why does food smell good?

Food smells good when it is safe to eat.

Fresh fruit and vegetables smell good. They are healthy to eat. When food smells bad, it might not be safe to eat.

Do a blindfold smell test. Can you name different fruits just by their smell?

A hammerhead shark smells blood and food in the water. Its nostrils are far apart on its strange head. This helps the shark find where a smell is coming from.

Bees are attracted to flowers by their color and smell. They feed on the flower's sweet nectar.

How do we taste?

We taste with our tongue,
but we use our nose as well.

Taste buds on our tongue tell us if food is sweet, sour, salty, or bitter. But to get the full flavor, we must smell food as we eat it.

Try a blindfold taste test. Can you guess the flavor of potato chips from their taste? Now pinch your nose gently. Is it harder to guess the flavor when you cannot smell?

Some animals taste with other parts of their bodies. An octopus tastes with its tentacles. When it touches something that tastes good, it pulls it into its mouth.

A mosquito tastes with its feet. When a mosquito lands on a human, it tastes the human's skin before biting and sucking out blood.

25

How can I take care of my senses?

You can take care of your senses in many ways. If you don't, they can easily be damaged.

Be careful when you use sharp objects. Never push them into somebody's eyes, ears, or nose.

When it is sunny, protect your skin with suntan lotion and wear a hat to shade your face. Never look directly at the sun.

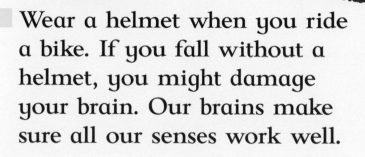

Wear a helmet when you ride a bike. If you fall without a helmet, you might damage your brain. Our brains make sure all our senses work well.

How do you think these things could damage your senses: computer screens, loud music, television? What can you do to protect your senses from them?

27

Glossary

Braille
A way of reading and writing. The letters are made from raised dots that a blind person can read by touch.

echo
A sound that bounces back to your ear. You can hear an echo when you clap near a cliff or in a cave.

nostrils
The two openings at the bottom of the nose. We breathe and smell though our nostrils.

prey
An animal that is hunted by another animal. When a fox hunts a rabbit, the rabbit is the fox's prey.

pupil
The black hole at the center of the eye that lets in light.

sensitive
Something is sensitive when it can feel, or sense in another way.

sign language
A language spoken using hand movements instead of words.

taste buds
Small bumps on our tongue that send messages to our brain to tell us how our food tastes.

tentacle
A long, bendy part of the body. Some animals feel and smell with their tentacles.

Index

Animal index and quiz

Use your animal index to find the answers to this animal quiz!

How many eyes do some spiders have?

How does an aardvark use its ears to catch ants?

How does a seal stay warm?

A bear can smell honey from far away. How far?

Which part of the body does an octopus use to taste?

Which senses does a mole use to find its way around underground?